RADIO TOOTH

RADIO TOOTH

PAUL JENKINS

FOUR WAY BOOKS
Marshfield

Editorial Office
Four Way Books
PO Box 607
Marshfield, MA 02050

Library of Congress Catalog Card Number: 96-86558

ISBN 1-884800-11-4

Cover design by Zuzzolo Graphics, Inc.
Text design by Acme Art, Inc.

Manufactured in the United States of America

This book is printed on acid-free paper.

Four Way Books is a division of Friends of Writers, Inc.,
a Vermont-based not-for-profit organization.

ACKNOWLEDGMENTS

My thanks to the editors of the following magazines and journals, in which some of the poems in this volume first appeared, several of them under different titles and in somewhat altered forms.
The Gettysburg Review: "Antietam"
Indiana Review: "How Animals Think" and "Class Phylum Kingdom"
The New Yorker: "Sister Agnes" and "This Horse"
The Marlboro Review: "Then We Started up into the Woods"
Ploughshares: "Headboard and Footboard"

Deep gratitude to Carlen Arnett, who made these poems better, and to Ellen Doré Watson, who makes everything better.

CONTENTS

1

2

"This is how man responds, this is how he responds to death,
this is how he looks forward and listens sideways,
this is how water, contrary to blood, is made of water,
this is how fire, opposite of ash, smooths its ruminant chills."
— César Vallejo
(tr. Clayton Eshleman and José Rubia Barcia)

"We went through the classes of insects
with their liquid liqueur-glass eyes.
He said, 'Nature's a shambles.
There's no vision. You're seeing for the last time.'"
— Osip Mandelstam
(tr. Clarence Brown and W.S. Merwin)

For my mother, who returns
And my father, who stays

1

VACANT LOT

These rooms are where we live but not for long
Across the fence a dog does its stations of the cross
Cigarette foil a dead shoe a clump of reddening sumac

If it's wholeness you want you better search somewhere else
And privacy and safety because all I know
Is there's less horizon every time I look

And I need that vacant lot more than my own daughter
I take it back she so chockful of promise
And joy but what is joy next to a battered shoe

Because nowhere in Genesis does it say one God alone
Omnipotent let alone even-handed
I love where the rival magicians arrive with their tents

Because a realtor in a Buick is crawling by very slow
Because there's no promise greater than promise unfulfilled
Because the cotton batting's bursting from a cast-off mattress

And I'm standing here without a reason in the world
Like the lilies of the field like a complete idiot
Hopping on one foot coaxing on the shoe

ORCHARD STREET

One block long and giant maples tall
Like a sleeve whose arm withdrew without a sound
Calm little street most patient of streets
That leads me out of myself then home

Past the first house on the left whose outsides turn
Salmon to mint green one more clapboard at a time

Past the second on the left not a house but a shipwreck

Past the shoebox on the right all alone
Perched on the riverbank like a realtor's nightmare
Past the man who says out loud
He's had too much to drink every day for forty years
And the woman flinging breadcrusts at the chickens

While on the left harmony regains the upper hand
Pinwheels pink geraniums frothing in their boxes
Past the bachelor brothers on the porch
Taking turns on the accordion that wheezes and soars
Until one goes in to the darkened kitchen
And a flashlight leads the other to the shed

Intimacy it's not what you think the last room
Down a hallway whose direction points further inward
It's these houses that can only hold so much before they spill
And this street that rhymes with wonder and chagrin
On alternating weekdays

Where everyone is turning odd myself included
Where to talk you stand not eye to eye but cheek to cheek
Staring off into open space like this

Past No. 5 where a cat lies napping and the blinds are always drawn

Past Mister Death himself
With his hound on a rope with his cheese-filled crackers
Who survived thirty-two years with buckshot in his skull
And when I pulled him from the rubble of the house trailer
Muttered nothing can kill me thanks anyway friend

Street that can't be a novel because it only leads back and forth
That doesn't need me to complete its story
That stretches past the fire pond then just ends
At the foot of my front lawn
Gazing back down its length like God's judgment

Because I have to know if we live
Ready or not in certain strangeness
Or in the paradise that is

ANTIETAM

Now that everyone's father is/was alcoholic
And the two Germanies merge at midnight like a woods
I refuse to be healed I refuse to love my neighbor
Or embrace the one true church like a boy his dog

You could see them camped on either bank of the stream
Under paper hats as if tomato seedlings might freeze
It is true what Davis thought of Lincoln
A lost calf bawling for its ma

In the name of union in the name of stand or fall
And the creek a midline between a brain's two lobes
And the bridge two thousand went to cross in waves
And all the hillside a storm surf of debris

How I detest the mathematics the language the snapping flags
The premise of oneness that passes for wisdom even now
As if the manic-depressive were a plot against the good
And the cross-dresser and the lotused self-immolator

Now that all our violence has lodged itself within
Like a fishbone in the windpipe or been exported overseas
So that innocence may survive innocence and the dream
Of the time we fought it out in the open and were made whole

PICTURE WINDOW

Happy but unhappy but what else
No telltale smell the photographs locked
In their gilt frames like stroke victims

Maybe the clot of butter on my bread
Maybe the shadow inching up the stairwell
It's dark in here and I forgot my stick of chalk

Maybe the words *thicker than water*
Like a bead of honey like a sorry noose
Followed by *it hurts me as much as it hurts you*

Don't ask me to explain I was barely there
As the prairie rolled through the picture window
And a jet trail melted like creation in reverse

While the grownups grew hard shells around their thoughts
And the houses played leapfrog the length of the street
Which dead-ended in a cornfield

Just how did back there lead to here
If I keep on going I'll never get far
Enough away or come full circle

Call it the ruthlessness of children
Call it a sonata composed
By the inexorable rules of music

Call it anything call it fear
But when I step inside the door
It's vanished again with its necessary secret

FOURTEEN STATIONS

He can be pitting cherries or laying bathroom tile
When a fresh wave of sorrow breaks over his head

How I envy the extremes the steep peaks the sudden troughs
Because he could not bear to see his parents sad

And because no one had bothered to bend down
To paint the underside of the dashboard

It's two in the afternoon the car is driving itself
And I'm drifting aimlessly the way bad monks think

Past a road crew sealing cracks with hot oil
Past a forlorn goose eyeing a sleeping dog

Past the tired cemetery where the three year old
Asks what's that little city made of teeth

Past the fractured guardrail my most sacred shrine
Where a car spun out then actually flew

Past the liquor-store-turned-Pentecostal-church
Past the baker in his hat white eyebrows white shoes

Past the Castaways Lounge where a creased dollar bill
Buys a minutes's gaze into her open secret

Does this sadness have an origin does any story suffice
Past the handwalker hand over hand along the wall

Until he reaches an intersection and suddenly makes a run for it
Unendurable no it's terrific it's a triumph

Past the framed photograph of my father in my mind
Who himself went ten rounds with depression and drew

God the Father the Son the Holy Ghost
Which scared the third-graders so badly their teacher
    substituted Spirit

Past the kidnappers' walk-up once more and again
Where my sister lived four days at the point of an icepick

And still we don't talk about it and still she plays Bach
Unswervingly by heart her eyes half closed

Past the point I know whether to weep or exult

SISTER AGNES

Perfect things don't need us
So I prune the rosebush steal an egg from beneath the hen
And set a cake pan under a weeping rafter

But Sister Agnes what about Sister Agnes
Who left the convent to its rooms
For a hut in the outback so small
She could only sleep standing up

Oh she was so gone
I cried three days in a row
For my own lack of

And when a plane winks overhead
Between the right thumb and forefinger
I squeeze a tiny dove aloft
To help bear up the heavy load

While Sister Agnes simply Sister Agnes
Leaves the door ajar when she's out
Walking or sleeping beside the haphazard cows

How could I leave this fat life
With its hearts of palm with its photo albums
The child still sorrowing over the lost hen
And Mama still lecturing her lupines in a dream

But Sister Agnes always Sister Agnes
Cannot be found at the moment I need her
After a drive of how many miles

The door wide open the biscuit on the table
Solid to the touch as through the glassless window
A cow gazes at me out of one side of its head

—for Adélia Prado

HEADBOARD AND FOOTBOARD

I call my father on the phone it's twenty years today
My mother died and his life turned sorry
And he's filing his fishing hooks smoothing down the barbs
He's going to throw back every bass in Minnesota

When Grandfather died death stood way over there
In a grey sharkskin suit directing the mourners
When the cars arrived back at the house
The cousins hid in the toolshed and dared each other to look

Death don't come any closer as it is
I'm having enough trouble separating things
Milk blooming across the floor where the child spilled it
My father's voice rising inside mine

As the two-way radio calls all EMTs
Subject with a gunshot wound to the head
And Ellen tosses on the first sweatshirt she can find
HEAVEN across her chest in raised letters

They describe a rushing a dark spiral then light
A dolphin in a net that springs a lucky hole
Or the recruit in real battle cradling his bad lap
Until his eyes widen whoops whoops there I go

Death who used to be so obvious the butcher and the blade
Who shaved the corpse a second time then poured another round
As subtle now as a stray thought
Or a slug melting in a slow pail of salt

In my mind as the marigolds blaze like new pennies
In my hands stacking cordwood in neat rows
In the heart that opens one pink valve at a time
In these words that are not words but stifled shouts

In the bed's carved headboard in the bare footboard too
In Ellen's sexual groans no never inside Ellen
In all that's too solid all that dissolves
Fear has always guided me to the things I love

ROUND AND ROUND

Then we started up into the woods
Along the path the deer make between spring and fall
So narrow even the dancer fell to either side

Then we started up into the woods
Which aren't speaking to me and my mind
Said tall ship said broom handle said machine guns on skis

Then we started up into the woods
Which still are the woods bless the standoff in court
Between the subdividers and loggers

Then we started up into the woods where the kids
Thrust their heads into knotholes into the owl's nest
Then spooked at the sight of the Cadillac's fins

Junked in a ravine and wouldn't look
At the seat coils the mouse fluff the bejeweled floorboard
Until we climbed back onto the trail and they stopped whimpering

Then we started up into the woods and the C4s
Came in low over the ridge weekend training for the Guard
At which the children began to gallop and sing

Then we started up into the woods and watched
Rocks in a streambed flicker then glow
Like the faces of those who know they are dying

While a catbird started up behind a leaf
As if the music of the last century were still being composed
They say it's too late but what do they know

Because in the woods I don't know what time it is
Because I can't for the life of me tell a story in a straight line
Because old cellar holes choked with sumac and hemlock

Because bears in caves their transmitters going strong
Because raccoons in the suburbs their dainty vicious feet
Because I forgot all about the wild children

Flipflopping between euphoria and dismay
Which is my question also and just because
Once I threw my boyish arms around a tree

Ringing out and out like an ocean in the dark
Because the trees won't remember because it's you and me
From now on and the tired kids lagging

Because the bunch of us started up into the woods
With nothing in mind except to keep the humdrum at bay
When the music started and here we go again

LUCKY CHALKBOARD

Not at all as they described it
Not a word about buttonholes or belt loops
On the suddenness of fireflies complete silence
No mention of the Smallest Chapel in the World

If it's spirit that transcends how was I to understand
My flesh rising through the bathwater's bubbles
And why Mother still studies her college reading list
And Father in the darkened room only she can enter

Maybe it's simply this dumb lumber my self
Rinsed clean each night like a lucky chalkboard
Or the knifeblade between shadow and light
Which the rooster won't cross fussing in the doorway

While the hens dart blithely in and back out
And a cow pokes its nose through the kitchen window
Then pans the back yard like a bank camera
If only I had listened to the advice

To take it as it comes to not ask why
They said nothing about time the intolerable wait
Or sweet fern underfoot or the Tilt-A-Wheel ride
Tipping us suddenly into giddiness

Or where Grandpa places the woolen sock at night
With the wooden leg snoring inside it
As if the ordinary weren't already too extraordinary by half
As if I weren't already lost to imagination

PARADISE

In this life not any other
Because the papaya tastes so entirely papaya
Because your nipples beneath the stretch-Lycra
Glow in daylight like a double eclipse
And because my neighbor took his loneliness in hand
And brought home a brace of llamas named Richmond and Mr. Chips

What could I want I don't already have
Maybe the howler monkey's Tibetan songbook
Maybe just a little more peace and quiet
To absorb creation's outrageous output
From a saint's thighbone to a blue minivan
And to draft my protest against the ban on Cuba

Because they're knocking at my door the Jehovah's Witnesses
With their white socks and drained faces
And their dire dream of kingdom-come at last
As the slaughtering goes on in a hundred dialects
For God for Allah for petroleum for the buzz
Of a bomber jacket and a pair of high-tops

Until I feel like kicking the cement
Because this world as it is because how can we stand it
In this life not any other

THE DEAD

Maybe they're coming back after all
Maybe they never fully left
Maybe the barrette she loved
The plastic one with purple grapes
An auburn strand still tangled in the clasp
Tugs at her like a little tide

Maybe the soul after all can't make a clean break
Maybe an ounce of fat still clings to the bubble
Maybe the blade grew dull
From all those generations scraping scraping
Or maybe too much weight in the ground
Keeps the craft from lifting

What if the dead are only lost to us
What if it's we who traveled so far
Inward there was no way out
What if deep inside our either/or
Infamous minds a lightswitch clicked
Stupidly between being and non-being

Because I've heard the voice bell-clear and hers
Because the catalpas are in full flower and I'm going a little nuts
Because she's waiting for me simply to crack open a window
Because bits of cotton fuzz cling to my father's ears
When he gets up from his nap and I know
He's frightened of his thoughts and of climbing stairs

Maybe there's no such thing as a higher good
Maybe baggy-necked moles tunneled out from under
Maybe the dead got sick of the ranked choirs
Singing perfect harmony and longed to hear
The catbird again the blab of tires against asphalt
Maybe there's no giving in at death's door

But a last abstraction after which we turn
Deft in the style that eludes me still
In the light that floods the sun-soaked laundry
In the edges of leaves in the composition scored
For cat gut and factory whistle
And in my thoughts always in my thoughts

WELL

Well the house cats were always sleeping
And the goats spent days inventing holes in the fence
And the bear came down only as far as the hives
And knocked their rocks off and scattered the sweet frames

Well the cats wandered to the screen door and complained
In unison and when I opened it decided not to
And the goats got up on top of each other no matter which kind
And the bear froze in the sheriff's searchlight

Well the cats set out within days of the U-Haul
And the son disappeared but the mother somehow found us
And the goats belonged to no one not then not ever
And the bear fell heavily to the ground and it took a winch

OUTBURST

Outskirts outbuilding outcast
And you want to go back there do you
Something I forgot something I mislaid
There's Mother with her topknot and her *Portia Faces Life*
There's Father with his eyes and his bronzed bust of Lincoln
There's my home town split down the middle like the brain
Blacks on one side of the river whites on the other
And the trailer park riding the prairie like a wave
And the fields ringing out like heartwood to the sky
And me split down the middle between love and hate
Like the river that won't heal itself

It's seven a.m. it's Thursday steady rain
Drips like a waterclock through the tent's weave
Anywhere I touch it solitude my wife
Empty sieve little sadsack giddy orphan one two three
And an orange salamander has wriggled in overnight
Clinging to the canvas touch-me-not touch-me
Its sides rhythmically filling and collapsing
As I touch it and nothing breathes

THEN WE STARTED UP
INTO THE WOODS

Then we started up into the woods
On horseback this time huge and unguarded
The pine needles red along their edges and cold
Crisscrossing the streambed like stitching a wound
When the trail veered off past a rusting chassis
That met my gaze head-on its headlights blown
Like a piglet born strange no jelly in the eye socket
And the infant on my chest began sobbing and couldn't stop

Oh little one will you ever grow used to it
Ruins stronger than all our strength to build
Condos that climb like stacking toys uphill
And the cement dome that caps the nuclear reactor
In the valley below when we reach the summit
Because it is left to us to be happy if we can
As the horses wander off cropping fistfuls of grass
And it's dusk already but the horses know the way down

2

MAP

On the way from my house to your house
Left up a short steep hill across a footbridge

On the way from my house to your house
At the reservoir's edge where the asphalt disappears

On the way from my house to your house
Butterflies the size of handkerchiefs orchids like soft stars

On the way from my house to your house
The dead mall cheek to cheek with the live mall

On the way from my house to your house
Be in the moment entirely starting now

On the way from my house to your house
Flying to the pale glow where your swimming suit has been

On the way from my house to your house
In the lead boots with scissors snicksnacking behind

On the way from my house to your house
If I loved you better would I get there sooner

On the way from my house to your house
Happy sad happy sad like a stupid lightswitch

On the way from my house to your house
I could find it in my sleep the river carried it away

On the way from my house to your house
What good is memory leading back the way it came

On the way from my house to your house
One lurch to quicken the other to delay

On the way from my house to your house
Every time the first time exorbitant scary

On the way from my house to your house
Like a pilgrimage of cripples like a marathon at night

On the way from my house to your house
Like the arrow that is always only halfway to its mark

Like a prayer flung out toward the vanishing horizon
On the way from my house to your house

THE NEXT NIGHT

Jessye Norman nails a high A through the roof of my head
A mouse is working in the wallboard I sealed its hole with duct tape
Della calls from the top of the stairs the cat is sleeping on her legs

A car drifts by without lights we're on a dead-end lane
The coyotes love the blue moonlight it's their wake-up call from the
    depths
Ellen pauses in her study the power still humming but the keyboard
    quiet

Comes a moment one hears everything sees everything
Like a witness to an execution
Who returns to life as from the other side

GOD'S KISSES

"If the flesh live for the sake of the spirit, it is
a miracle. But if the spirit for the sake of the body,
it is a miracle of a miracle."
                        —The Gospel According to St. Thomas

Maybe she would like them Augustine claims
They take forever to begin even longer
A dry feather against the lips then the slightest pull
The tip of the tongue too intimate for words
Then the vowel the full syllable the diphthong

I concentrate on her being on her erotic soul
And the twin saltcellars along her tanned shoulders
When the word *furrow* arrives and unhinges me entirely
Pinned against the desktop again in seventh grade
Or like the puzzled toddler look my penis is fishing

Lust it's the puffed-up baritone's high A
So exorbitant *Don Giovanni* suddenly turns tragic
No it's a bulldozer and a shantytown on its knees
No it's the 26th of July the sky deep green
And I'm restless as a telephone and her sundress is sleeveless

This lust that still holds us at arms' length
After our souls those old Balkans lowered their gates
Cruel jest it was our bodies knew each other first
Strawberries reddening on our knees where we burned against the
    rug
Now her a great foreignness and me turned bold

Or not bold enough or how else
Explain the mystery of the body greater even than the mind's
As we who once lived for each other's lips
Add caution to our voices layers around our pearls
Daring each other to open up

HOW ANIMALS THINK

I may look like a pallbearer but I'm thinking about the day
A woman's skirt rode up two seats down at the movies
What is that ground squirrel thinking over there
Twitching above its hole
Like a seismograph inside a walnut

Does the pastor really believe the bodies will be raised
Does the elephant herd one year to the day
Return weeping to the bone pile and wildly trumpet
And the dog panting inside the closed car
Taste the rabbit it ate for breakfast all but the ears

I am trying to remember anything I can
About the dearly departed how her skinny arms
Flew up from her sides at the mere mention of naked
While the horse pastured beyond the trees
Tosses its head furiously then gallops off

I try concentrating on the undertaker's shoes
And the crumbs of soil on the plastic carpet
As the hole opens its dark chute
Into the stairless basement and who
Was that woman and why didn't I move down

THE END OF THE END OF

The toddler bounces up down up down and squeals
It's a party it's a party as the grownups clap
Until I carry her kicking off to bed

Back downstairs the current has drifted to the end
Of wilderness of history of the century the wine
Bottles like glowing strangers in our midst

Until everyone grows silent the muffled flap
Of footsoles on the stairsteps there she is
Grinning goofily above us all alive inside her skin

SONNET WITHOUT PAUSE

The lovers love gazing at the ocean at night
Love because that's what lovers do they have to
Or they aren't lovers anymore and the phone rings late
Love gazing because someone's unspooled yards and yards of foil
And the moon has a little dustcap tied behind her ears
As the ocean collapses in a heap then rebuilds
As he has as she has and with a little luck
They will keep taking turns not both fail at once
At night because that's when all the boundaries melt
For a long moment until the cloudbank passes
As she pulls on her sweater she's started to be cold
After sixteen years to be lovers still
The sawgrass nicking their heels as the crickets fall
Silent as they pass then whir up again

CLASS PHYLUM KINGDOM

Mrs. Elliott said thinking in a straight line
Proves you were born a rung higher than monkeys
And round handwriting shows you are well-adjusted
As I dreamed of Sue Zwanziger under the baseball stands

Does my life still love me
A loud bawling all night long
And this morning a new calf sprawled in the field
As a coyote inches over the rise

To be intent on one thing and one thing alone
While the hens keep doing their hapless thing
Playing masters and slaves as their glass eyes
Spot a hawk on an updraft who turns down

As the stallion whinnies and whinnies in loneliness
Now that they've separated it from the roan colt
And I don't know why but I know
Fear is drawing closer cheek to cheek

MIRACLE OF A MIRACLE

Like one who has to see the nail holes to believe
I linger near the miracle of her body
With its solid-to-the-touch with its shy indifference
With its visible scars on both forehead and lip
Where a dog's teeth clamped down and where the car accordioned
And the sickle-shaped one where the half-born sat up and waved

Disquisitions on the soul that whirligig forgive me
But I haven't yet described the splendor of the flesh
Let alone its lasting promise
Until I arrive at the places her bikini has been
The inner lips peeking shyly out then less shyly
Her cleft a niche with a little live saint perched inside

No graven images echoes somewhere in my head
And me smack-dab against the fact of her being
With its borders like the border guard who looked the other way
With its rabbit's foot that glistens as it's stroked
And its monk's hood and its sudden whiplash
When I am so far inside it hurts

Otherness you're the only god I need
Because the object of my love is an inexhaustible subject
Because the soul is three walnut shells and a pea
Already rehearsing its final disappearance
Because what I thought was far away is very near
Until miracle of a miracle my foreignness brushes hers

THIS WAY THEN THAT WAY

The chipmunk comes to table then scurries off in high fear
Is the world going to turn out friendlier or much nastier

When coyotes begin caroling on the next hill
The voices say menace then giddy champagne

When I'm lost in the mind of the stunned sheep
It's like river barges someone forgot to couple

Drifting without a pilot leisurely downstream
Until next morning the chipmunk reappears

On the picnic table all contrariness and nerve
Jerking this way then that way

This way then that way like the seasick song
The toddler wants over and over again and dances

THIS HORSE

Muzzle like a shoe on a shoe last
Legs like cocked rifles
And they say the miracle's not the body but the soul

Into that oblong sheath
Slips a dagger of thought
As out from its gaze it bursts into full stride

Now it lingers at the far end of the field
Neck down nose down
A magnified flea

When I draw close it looks up
An entire orchestra poised for the downbeat
My own chest the drum

Thudding and repeating
It's got your number you don't have a clue
And

This horse is real
Unlike us whose glory will have been
We longed to exist beyond ourselves

RAIN FOREST

The leaf-cutter ants are the fishing fleet's sails
You can hear the monkeys long before you see them
Crashing through the canopy white faces squeezed
Into skullcaps ribbed like walnuts
I'm a blind man listening for the first time to his ears
No I'm a nervous system doing handstands

The deluge arrives between five and seven
All night into next morning like the first day of the world
Land where they say the devil lost his boots
Where United Fruit Co. lost its shirt
When the banana groves mildewed when the price of palm oil slid
As the rain starts out in D then layers up E and F

As creatures begin slipping through the windows' fretwork
Under a tile roof our refuge spiders wide as my fist
Birds that warble like water glasses in a vaudeville act
Grasshoppers long as tongue depressors a neighbor's dog
So thin it squeezes between the bars as cicadas rev
Their starting-line engines a foot from our heads

As the rain goes on drumming its own dance of mayhem
Two by two two by two let creation in
Through the window holes the doorways the chinks in ourselves
We've patched with privacy with caution with baling wire and twine
Until the ark lets go its grip on the hill
And the wind wants to take place inside us like music

3

OCTOBER

When my legs are bald as an egg when I mistake my daughter
For my mother I will not be serene I'll argue with the doctors
And lurch in and out of clarity like a radio in a storm

Cricket behind the bookcase it's my hard time of year
When the light hangs glassy when the maples let go
And the far ridge bristles like a banner in Arabic

Remember childhood when the world was obvious as an apple
And the grownups lingered talking behind their hands
No we were never innocent not even then

Inside the wall something rustles like a stage curtain
Then claws at the sheetrock as if a mineshaft had collapsed
And suddenly I'm holding onto life by my teeth

"WHAT YOU THINK
CAN'T HAPPEN CAN'T"

– Chinese fortune cookie

When it comes let it come with pennants in its hair
Like a used-car lot in June like a stadium scoreboard
When it comes let it come in an eighteen-wheeler
Studded with green and yellow lights like an onrushing arcade
With *Deus Me Livre* stenciled above the grille
And a vanity plate in back *Kiss Me Until It Hurts*

From the inside out that's how death prefers to work
Like an ad campaign for an insipid beer
You mute-button between innings and later that week
Find that very brand in your very own refrigerator
Or like the skin around my mother loose as a purse
As her eyes began to sink and her spleen ripened

Bad cell bad karma bad faith bad hat
I want my death out there where I can see it
Not lurking within this poem frightens me
Like St. Thomas's hand like a plane entering a cloud
And if what you think can't happen can't
Let it come right now right now or not ever

THE CHILD

Hops on one leg wrestles with my neck and inquires
Do animals have spirits do cars
And why do chairs always live next to walls
Happy happy happy happy
Unhappy only if I refuse
The umpteenth refrain of *Alice the Camel*
Then inconsolable down to her toes
When the thumbed-down eye of the doll won't open
Or when the nestling robin's neck lolls
So I'm here to soften the extremes a bit
So I'm here to thumb the eyelid up
To lie and to hold
A hole in my head the size of October
A tightness in the chest two miners since dawn
Inching between the mineshaft's rubble

WHAT CHEER

Rake off last year's garden and a new crop of stones
Has worked its way through the topsoil inexhaustible champagne

I'm down in the darkness with the baggy neckless moles
Pushing earthballs through tunnels with their felt-tipped noses

And with my ancestors undermining Wales
With their burlap sacks and blackened faces

And their headstones in What Cheer Iowa still
Where coal ribboned beneath all that corn

Veins crossing recrossing the shallow hills
Then turning in under the ignorant houses

I have that rasp in my breathing that twisted shoulderblade
And that habit of being joyless when I first sit down

Which say I was born to dig born to root and poke
Because I love the smack of the spade because these buoyant stones

Aren't stones at all but self-excavating moles
Rising through the soil like blind hope

What Cheer with neither question mark nor exclamation
So they could have it both ways and so can I

THE ABANDONED
SLAUGHTERHOUSE

If you let your eyes rest for a moment in the dark
A little light hovers above the stainless tables
Hooks hanging from the rails then the walk-in freezer
If you can force yourself through the gaping door

If you let your mind go you can hear the pink slabs
Singing along the ceiling as the black hoses snort
And the floor drain gulps and even the report
Of the pistol in the holding pens out back

Oh the world seemed so obvious in fourth grade
The field trip to the packinghouse and every spring thereafter
So we could follow what our fathers the farmers began
And lend a hand with the hoeing and the haying

And see the fate of meatpackers in little knots
Smoking in the parking lot their T-shirts cut
Off below the nipple as a pinkish cloud
Drifted east or west from the lone chimney

Now I'm gazing deeper into the gloom
As fear tugs one way fascination the other
Fear of what fear of whom if I knew
Would I be standing here trembling at the door

JOURNEY TO THE DEAD

Can't get there from here you have to pass
Back through the eye of the very same needle
Pulling your little length of thread

A big broom must have scattered the marigold petals
Or maybe the orator's grand words
Enough to choke the candles

Them on their side me on mine
That's how we prefer it
That's what we agreed

Except a thin wire of sound
Keeps scritching inside the chapel's lightbulb
Which frightens the child but excites me

As if the fences between us were about to fail
As if the war between the ranchers and the shepherds
Had the shepherds winning this time for good

Once you had to go on foot
Following a dolphin in a rickshaw
To the groaning pier and tousle a dwarf's hair

Then pour a beaver of blood into the dark hole
Until their faces took on a little rose
And their tongues loosened between their clenched teeth

Now I'm riding the F train between 12th and Chambers
When a girl beside me on her way to school
Cups her hands to the glass and says there look

The abandoned station and swears
She's seen figures moving in the inky dark
And I cup my palms just in time

Now I'm tubing the Deerfield River with Charles
Who sees the surface flatten ahead
And says his dead brother loved this stretch

Says he's here right now feel the current within the current
As my chest goes a little nuts and the boyish name
She used to call me rushes between my ears

In that grass-green dress in the hand-painted frame
When I concentrate harder still
The image blurs then vanishes completely

Over there for good
That's what we agreed to
Back the way she came

NAMING NAMES

It was you Alfred who had to lead
Into then out of the belly of fear

And you Donald on the front porch
On a hot July night with your dim brother
Wrong notes and all as the accordion wheezed

And you Nina bone-white as the sheets
In the study-turned-sickbay your head half turned
Paul I'm going to make it I don't know

And you in the square in the starched shirt
As the lead tank approached feinting feinting
To the right to the left like a duende's taunt

Who say I'm less solidly in this life than I claimed
So embarrassed I can feel my ribcage hammer

ORPHANS AND ANGELS

Have deserted their centuries to find us
Streaming once more from red brick mills
Prying gauzy wings from chapel ceilings

One has a violin case tucked underneath its arm
One weeps into a tin bowl
They find me at a truckstop on my second coffee

Maybe they believe I'm the one who called
Maybe they're just lollygagging
Until the odometer can heave up the century's O's

So they can begin all over from the word scratch
The treadmill of sadness and consolation
With their sun-drenched linen their voluptuous tears

Listen I've had it up to here
With absence-inside-presence with bric-a-brac wings
Trailing lightly down the nearest shoulder

Because the only true orphan lost its shadow in a fire
Because the one true angel faces the other direction
Because it falls to us to keep the invisible at bay

And I refuse to be sad or saved

POWER (1)

Not enough to go around
So the gods feuded and one big god emerged

Not enough to go around
So the forest disappears and the wolves are on the move

Not enough to go around
So a black man wears a tire around his neck and a white man gold

Not enough to go around
Said the boss to the employee said the spider to the moth

Not enough to go around
A friendship dissolving over a drowned boat

Not enough to go around
The volume is too loud turn it down

Crickets throbbing in the corners little Neros in a fire
The papery maple leaves on fire

And I can't find that tiny place inside
Where there's enough (prove it) to go around

POWER (2)

Too low in the sky comes a plane
Two more at its wingtips like paperdolls holding hands
I'm caught in the crosshairs or else
They're just boys hotdogging on weekends

Jump up on the picnic table and shake my fist
Or dash inside and dial the airbase
The heron I surprised this morning in the pond
Trailed its legs like cocktail forks as it rose

Remember the chart on the schoolroom's wall
With its wider tree trunk and tapering branches
On which the improving animals sat
From the opossum way up to the human

And the afternoon in fourth grade
Jimmy Cheevers stood between the doorway and bus
And wouldn't let me pass and I hid
In the darkened lunchroom until the janitor found me

To which the judo master suggested learn to yield
Along the line of least resistance then a sideways blow
Which sweet poetry amended to control and be controlled
By turning always turning

As the planes return for a second pass
Even lower this time I can see the cockpit's
Smoked glass and straining rivets
And nothing will save us not even rage

POWER (3)

In the secret in the shout in the rotunda in the weave
In mystery in candor in chanting in silence
In the cricket in the cricket cage in the nighthawk the word alone
In the highway that divides the pasture in two
In the footpath that shadows the river's every move

In the slaughterhouse the millpond the flying shuttle the silk
In the demagogue the dissident in magnetism in ruin
In the pipe organ's ranks in its forest of tall straws
In the two-year-old's lips rounding the word *now*
In the fourteen-year-old's *fuck you*

In the hermit in the President when they enter each other's dreams
In the windsock that fills and just as suddenly empties
In life that is constantly reinventing itself
In league with death who urges faster faster
In music that undoes me whether I say yes or no

In the door that's balky in the door that simply yields
In mastery that masters then ends up drunk in a motel
In ruins stronger than all my strength to count
In memory thereof in forgetting also
In the stubborn detail that eludes them both

In a hurry in tandem in jest in resolve
In the name of bellowing from the nearest roof
In the either/or that cancels neither
In the prayer that carries nearly thirty miles
In an instant and enters the fat tumor's cells

In surprise in ongoingness in weakness as much as strength
In the mind's imitation of the gods' glibness
In sorrow in permanence in giddiness in short
In the same quandary I was stuck in yesterday
In the face of all there is to lose

RADIO TOOTH

You have to stop searching
Until you find it
The borrowed woodcut buried all that year
A black Madonna in a peasant skirt
In the entire house nowhere
Its owner begging its return

Until one night flying low above the floor
A little trickier through the doorframes
When I woke there she was in the very drawer

Or like the crystal set built in youth
Wrapping a toilet-paper tube with copper wire
The crystal gleaming like a silver molar
The night sky salted with stars
When I could hardly stand the hissing in my ears
The static weakened to a thread of music

Look with all your eyes
Listen with your bad tooth aching
Something's out there

Paul Jenkins teaches poetry and poetry writing at Hampshire College and is editor of *The Massachusetts Review*. Father of two daughters, he lives with his wife, the poet and translator Ellen Doré Watson, in Conway, Massachusetts. His first book, *Forget the Sky,* appeared from L'Epervier in 1980.